This Big Talkabout book is full of attractive, colorful and interesting pictures which will provide hours of enjoyment for your child. We know that the early growth of language and an ever widening vocabulary are very important for a young child and this book has been specially planned to cover most of the areas which will be helpful to your child before he or she goes to school.

You will help your child by using the pages in this book for talking with him or her. On each page, a short question or title has been given to help you. There are no particular answers to most of the questions because it is more important that your child should just talk about the pictures. By talking with him you can help him relate the pictures to the things he knows from his own experience. For example, in the section called 'Have you heard these?' – first you might ask the child what is the name of each of these things which makes a noise. Then show him how clapping hands make a sound, and let him do it with you. Can he remember the noise the vacuum cleaner makes when you are cleaning? What other things make different sounds? You could talk about the sound of the cars and trucks passing by outside. Most children these days recognize the sound of a police car or fire engine siren. What about things which only make a little noise? Let your child talk about the sounds he can make, like splashing in the bath, knocking at the door and creeping up the stairs without making a sound.

On the last page there are some further suggestions on how you can extend the use of this picture book with games and activities which your child will enjoy.

Acknowledgment:
The photographs and endpapers are by Hurlston Design Ltd.

Copyright © 1978 Ladybird Books Ltd.
Copyright © 1981 Modern Promotions
Copyright © 1985, 1989 Modern Publishing, a division
of Unisystems, Inc.

PRINTED IN BELGIUM

my first big talkabout book

with illustrations by
Harry Wingfield, Martin Aitchison and Eric Winter

MODERN PUBLISHING
A Division of Unisystems, Inc.
New York, New York 10022

fun with color

Which colors are the same?

Talk about the colors

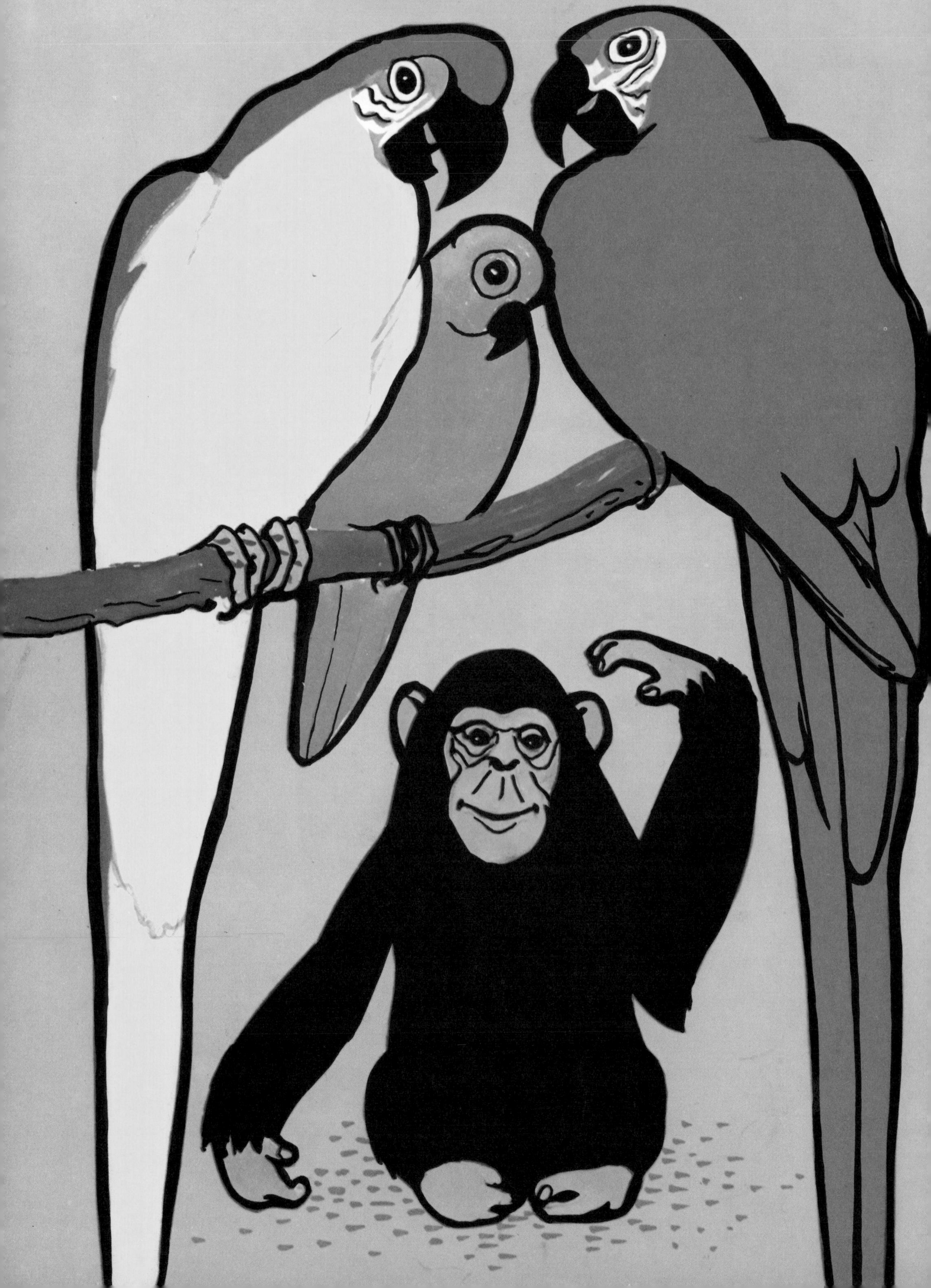

look and find

Where does each
piece fit?

**Find one
the same
as this**

. . . and this

. . . and this

. . . and this

Match the picture
with the shape

Which shop sells these?

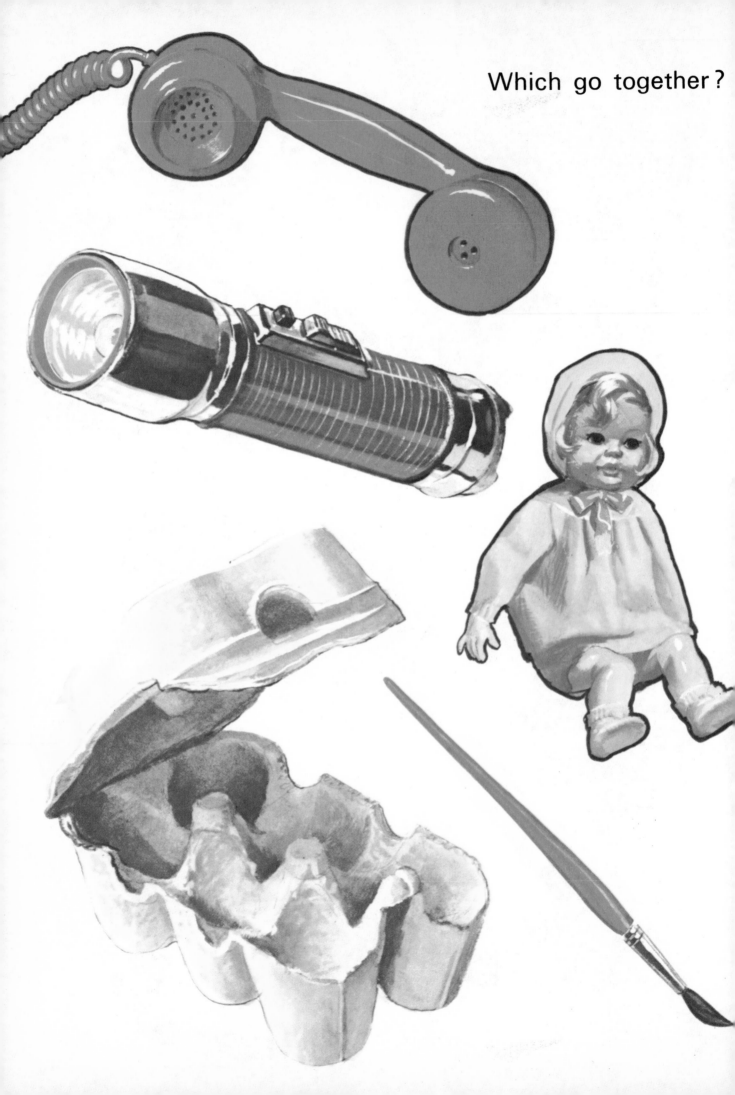

Which go together?

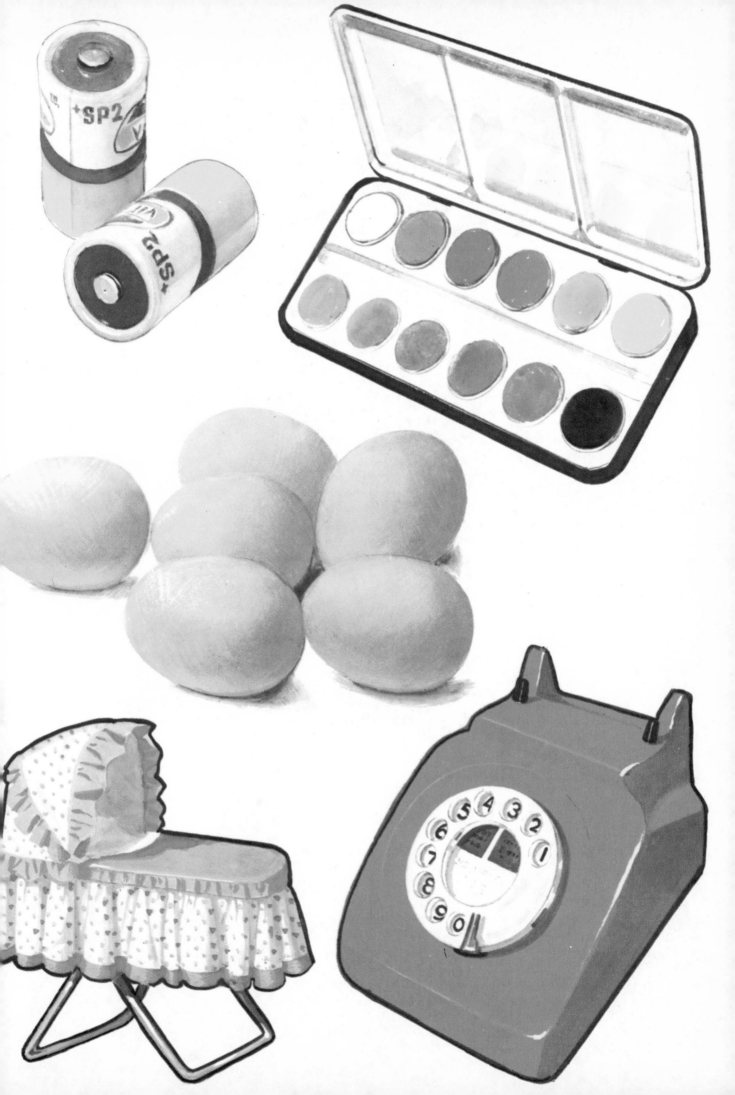

using your senses

Have you **felt** these?

Have you **seen** these?

What noise does each animal make?

Have you **tasted** these?

Have you **smelled** these?

Have you **heard** these?

picture puzzles

Who catches the fish?

Who owns which dog?

looking
at
nature

Can you name these animals and birds?

Rabbit

Fish

Guinea Pig

Cat

Gerbil

What are
these pets called?

Talk about the hungry birds

What is in the yard?

What is above and below the ground?

Spring

Summer

Autumn

Winter

Talk about the whole year

tell me a story

Who gets wet?

Tell the 'long dog' story

What happens in this story?

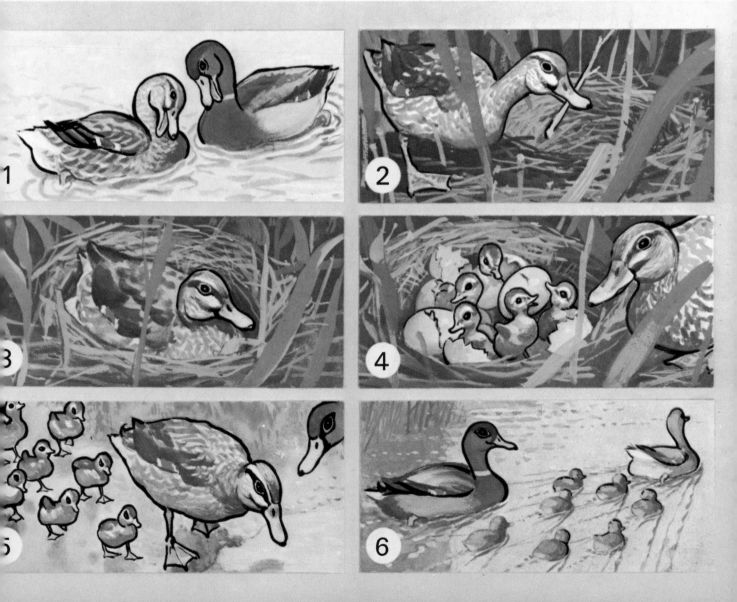

Do you know the story of The Three Little Pigs?

The early worm catches the bird

Who wins the race?

1

2

3

4

What is happening?

A fisherman's story

Tell the story of the bird-perch

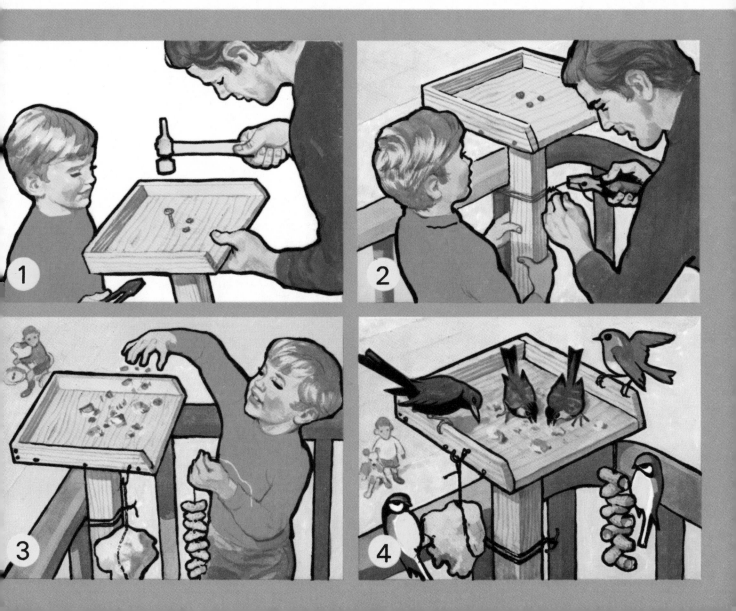

opposites

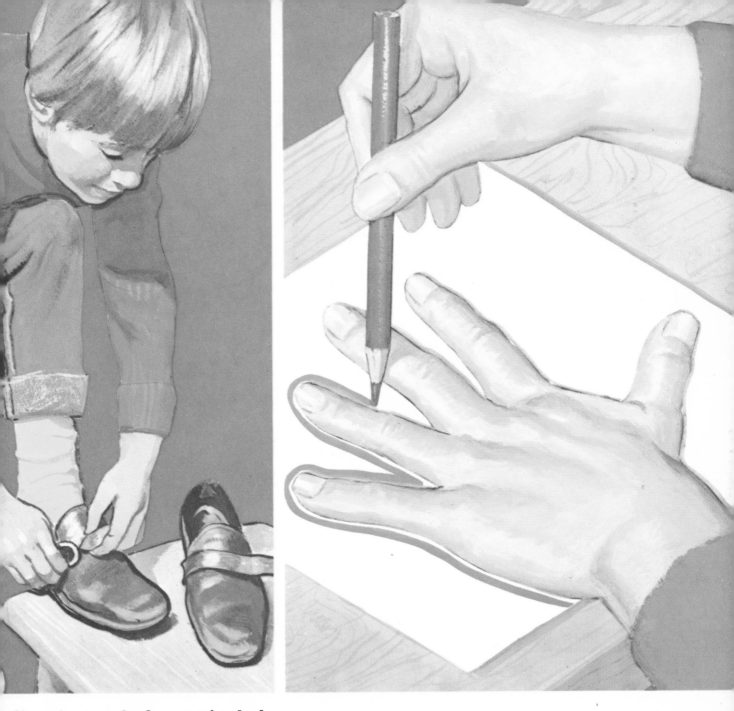

Talk about **left** and **right**

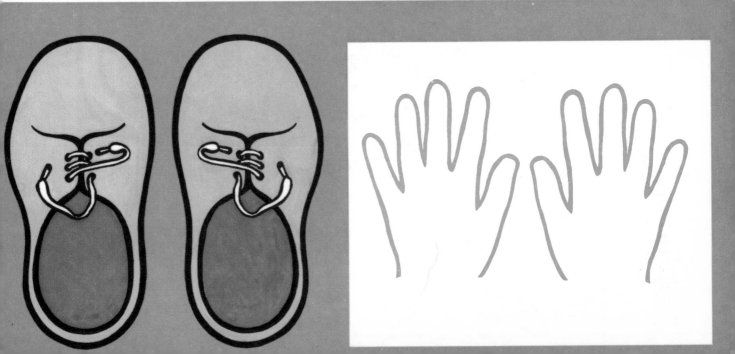

Which animals are **fast** and which are **slow**?

Talk about **big** and **little**

learn to count

1

2

3

4

5

How many eggs?

Count the buttons

1

2

3

4

5

6

Find another number like this 4

2 1 4

. . . and this

3 5 8 3

. . . and this

6 9 6 7

. . . and this

2 1 2 5

How old are you? Can you point to the number?